An  Management Briefing

An Introduction to Direct Marketing

Chaman L. Jain
Al Migliaro

**A Division of
American Management Associations**

Library of Congress Cataloging in Publication Data

Jain, Chaman L
   An introduction to direct marketing.

   (An AMA management briefing)
   Bibliography: p.
   1. Marketing. 2. Direct selling. 3. Adver-
tising. Direct-mail. I. Migliaro, Al, joint
author. II. Title. III. Series: American
Management Associations. An AMA management briefing.
HF5415.125.J34   658.8   78-4184
ISBN 0-8144-2218-7

Third Printing

Contents

About the Authors

Chaman L. Jain is currently Professor in the College of Business Administration, St. John's University, Jamaica, New York. He has been involved in direct marketing for 20 years, first as a director of economic research of the Epilepsy Foundation, and then as research consultant for such firms as Rapp & Collins, Bilgore Groves, Alexander Sales Corporation, and Union Fidelity Life Insurance Company. Dr. Jain holds a Ph.D. in Economics from The American University and an M.A. in Business Administration from Vanderbilt University. He has published a number of articles, both in professional and trade publications.

Al Migliaro is president of Glenwood Associates, Inc., Narberth, Pennsylvania, marketing and advertising consultants who specialize in direct marketing. Prior to launching his own firm in 1971, Mr. Migliaro was vice-president of marketing for Union Fidelity Life Insurance Company and managing editor of *The Magazine of Direct Marketing*. His career in the communications industry spans a period of 35 years, 25 of which have been in marketing and advertising.

Foreword

DIRECT MARKETING has long been neglected by top management executives for the simple reason that they have never fully understood its broad usage in today's business world. This briefing should go a long way toward correcting that situation and filling the information gap. As a practitioner in the field for many years, I have often wished there were something I could offer to corporate executives to tell them a little bit more about this unique method of marketing. Dr. Jain and Mr. Migliaro fulfill this need in this briefing.

Milton Smoliar
Director, Names Unlimited, Inc.

Acknowledgment

THERE are many people to whom the authors are indebted for much of what appears in this briefing, some of whom are mentioned in the bibliography and some of whom are among our previous employers and clients who allowed us to test many notions. We wish, however, to convey a special word of gratitude to James Connell, of Washington, D.C., at whose knee we first learned about the challenging, wonderful world of direct marketing. A special word of thanks also to Rosemarie Realmuto, who typed the manuscript, and to Gregory Pizzigno, research assistant.

Introduction

DIRECT MARKETING is a method of selling and distributing products or services. The relationship between buyer and seller and the action sought from the buyer by the seller are the two major factors that distinguish *direct* marketing from other forms. The following example will demonstrate this difference.

Auto makers market their automobiles through dealerships. Their national advertising efforts are directed toward creating desire and enticing people to visit dealerships. The sale is consummated when the prospective buyer visits a dealership and engages in a one-to-one relationship with a salesperson. In this instance the manufacturer does not have a direct link to the prospect.

If an auto manufacturer were to market its automobiles through direct marketing, its advertising would ask prospects to place orders directly with the company, either by mail or phone. The orders would be filled by the factory (or a regional warehouse), and the cars would be delivered directly to the homes of buyers. This description of direct marketing constitutes a narrow definition of the concept.

A broader definition of direct marketing includes any advertising or promotional effort directed toward obtaining responses, regardless of their nature (for example, personal visit to retail outlets, requests for literature, participation in contests through retail outlets). The only criterion that has to be met for such efforts to be included in the more inclusive definition is that the advertiser compile a list of respondents' names for future use. Also included in the broader definition of direct marketing is any project that involves direct mail, even if no direct response is solicited (for example, distribution of cents-off coupons).

Much of the material in this briefing is applicable to the activities that make up the broader definition of the concept. Specific references to, and detailed descriptions of, such activities are excluded from the discussion because of space limitations. Readers whose functions include any of the activities covered by the broad use of the term will recognize the applicable material and be able to adapt it to their specific needs.

However, it should be kept in mind that direct marketing, as used in this briefing, describes a situation in which the seller solicits orders from prospects, and the prospects place orders (by phone or mail) directly with the seller who, in turn, ships the products or services directly to customers from his own stock or through a third party (drop shipment).

It should also be pointed out that "direct mail" and "direct marketing" are not synonymous: Direct mail describes a medium of advertising, whereas direct marketing is a method of selling and distribution. Although this dichotomy is obvious to many practitioners, some confusion exists, even among professionals.

This is not to say that direct mail does not play an important role in direct marketing or that it is not a unique medium, for it does and it is. In recognition of these factors, this briefing devotes one full section to various aspects of direct marketing as they relate to all types of media, including direct mail, and a second section to those aspects of direct mail that set it apart from other media. Section 3 takes a peek into the future of direct marketing.

WHY DIRECT MARKETING?

Virtually every type of business and industry uses direct marketing because it is a profitable way of doing business. It is used to sell to business and industry, as well as to the general public. Direct marketing benefits both the marketer and the consumer. It is beneficial to the marketer because advertising cost-effectiveness is measurable in precise dollar terms, as is demonstrated in this briefing. The major advantage to consumers is the convenience of shopping at home at a desk, unharried by crowds, parking problems, and salespeople.

Much of the recent growth of direct marketing stems from three major factors: the influx of women into the labor force, who consequently have less time to shop; the increase in the number of people over the age of 65, many of whom prefer to shop by mail; and the expansion of credit cards. Until the advent of credit cards, most direct marketing offers required either cash payment with the order or COD. The credit card revolution eliminated the fear of buying by mail. The new message became: "You don't have to pay for it if it isn't delivered."

CAN YOU USE DIRECT MARKETING?

Your product line and company should meet certain criteria if direct marketing is to be used successfully. Here are ten questions you should be able to answer affirmatively if you are to succeed in direct marketing:

1. Does your product require frequent replacement? If not,
2. Is your product line broad enough to trigger frequent purchases, or does it lend itself to a continuity program? If neither 1 nor 2,
3. Can you price a single item high enough to support the promotional effort required, yet still realize a sufficient profit on one sale per customer to make the entire venture economically feasible?
4. Is the market large enough to make it possible to take advantage of the available economies of scale? If not,
5. Can your product line be repackaged, redesigned, repositioned, or all three, to broaden the market?
6. Are media that reach the target available and, if so, are they available at an economical cost?
7. Are your products easy to describe and demonstrate?
8. Can your products be delivered to individual buyers through available means of transportation (United Parcel Service, United States Postal Service, common carrier) at a

cost that allows you to establish a total price to the customer that is competitive?

9. Does the quality of your product or service stand up under an unconditional money-back guarantee?
10. Does your company have sufficient capital resources to wait a year, or perhaps two to five years, for a return on investment?

Even if your product represents a technological breakthrough that meets a genuine unfilled need touched by no other product on the market, you would still have to answer most of these questions in the affirmative to succeed. The significance of these questions will be more apparent as you read this briefing. If you can answer yes to most of the above questions, the chances are good that your company can launch a successful direct marketing program.

WHAT'S SO DIFFERENT ABOUT DIRECT MARKETING?

The elements that shape the development of marketing and advertising strategies in direct marketing are similar to those in other forms of marketing. The differences are a matter of emphasis and perspective. The direct marketer's objective is to acquire individual, identifiable customers for future profits, whereas the marketer whose product line is distributed through retail channels (the "general marketer") seeks to create customers as well, but identifies them as members of a group (market segment).

The direct marketer measures success in terms of the acquisition of identifiable customers and their value over time. The general marketer's success is tallied according to the degree of brand or product awareness, identification, acceptance, and loyalty among market segments translated into sales volume over the product life cycle. The direct marketer positions the company's products chiefly through selection of media, because, in the words of Frank Vos, "the medium is the market." The general marketer achieves this goal primarily through the selection of retail outlets. Pricing is of equal concern to both in positioning a product or brand.

Cumulative effect, recall, and awareness play a very small role in the direct marketer's lexicon. Each and every promotional effort, whether it be a mailing to one list, an individual print ad, or a series of commercials in broadcast, stands on its own. Each must produce a predetermined number of orders to be deemed successful.

Given the many similarities, anyone with a solid background in other forms of marketing should have no difficulty in developing marketing and advertising strategies for direct marketing. The degree of success will depend on the ability to adopt a different perspective in planning and carrying out these strategies.

We cannot pretend to make the reader an expert in direct marketing, for this briefing couldn't possibly cover everything one needs to know about the subject. It is, as the title suggests, an introduction to direct marketing. What we do hope to achieve through this briefing is:

1. To help the general marketer adapt his or her present knowledge to direct marketing.
2. To outline methods that can be used to incorporate direct marketing into the existing structure of companies engaged in general marketing.

1

Fundamentals
of Direct Marketing

CUSTOMER COST AND VALUE

THE direct marketer has two primary goals: to acquire customers, and to generate repeat sales from customers. In direct marketing it is recognized that most or all profit is derived from repeat sales to customers. The cost of acquiring customers as well as the value of the customers are two important concepts used to launch and operate a successful direct marketing enterprise and to establish the market value of an existing operation.

Customer Defined

There are three categories of customers in direct marketing: (1) active, (2) inactive, and (3) former. An *active* customer is anyone who has made a purchase within a specified period of time. If the time elapsed since the most recent purchase exceeds a certain period, the customer is characterized as *inactive*. The elapsed time varies with each operation, usually anywhere from 18 months to three years. There is no time period in insurance, magazine subscriptions, and other products or services that the customer can elect to cancel. Customers become inactive upon cancellation.

A customer enters the *former* category when repeated attempts at reactivation (offers to buy or renew) fail. The names and addresses of active, inactive, and former customers constitute the major part of the house list — a direct marketer's chief asset. Another segment of the house list is made up of *inquirers* — people who have shown an interest in the products or services, but who have not made a purchase.

Customer Acquisition Policy

Before a customer acquisition program can be undertaken, top management must adopt a basic policy to serve as a guide to marketing management. The policy establishes what methods will be used to acquire customers. The three different policies used are: maximum cost-recovery period, profit aspiration, or return on investment.

Maximum Cost-Recovery Period

Management may decide to establish the maximum period of time over which the cost of acquiring customers must be recovered from profits. This is relatively simple for an existing operation, for which past experience provides the guide. A new venture will establish the period in relation to the capital resources the company wishes to commit to bring the enterprise to a self-sustaining level. It can be as short as six months or as long as five years.

Here is an example of how this policy can be established for a new venture: Management allows a maximum period of three years for customer acquisition costs to be recovered. The three-year limit is determined by a combination of management philosophy, customer activity under current marketing methods, and industry data. Small-scale tests are conducted in selected *media vehicles** to get an indication of the actual average cost per customer. Manage-

*The terms *media type* and *media vehicle* are used in this briefing to avoid the ambiguity of the word *medium*. *Media type* refers to a group of media with a common characteristic (for example, all daily newspapers constitute a media type, as do all television stations, all magazines, and all billboards). *Media vehicle* refers to a specific entity within a group (for example, The New York Times, Ladies Home Journal, WNBC-TV—a television network also constitutes a media vehicle). The term *media type* can also refer to a group of media vehicles whose common characteristic identifies a broader or narrower group. *Print media*, which encompasses all media types that are printed, is an example of the broader group, while *shelter magazines*, which encompasses all magazines devoted to the domestic arts, is an example of the narrower group.

12

ment then forecasts how long it will take to recapture the cost on the basis of the profit contributed by an average customer for each year following acquisition. This establishes customer value. Methods for computing the cost of acquiring a customer and customer value are described later in this section.

Profit Aspiration

Under the profit aspiration policy, management is required to determine the profit, expressed in dollars, it desires from the operation at the end of a selected time period. As pointed out earlier, all profit is derived from promotions to customers. Projections are made as they are under the maximum cost-recovery period policy for new ventures, and are made on the basis of past experience in the case of existing operations. But the profit aspiration policy places the emphasis on how many customers have to be acquired over the time period to achieve the established profit goal. Whether the goal can be achieved is determined by the cost of customer acquisition and the customer value.

If, for example, management decrees a profit goal of $800,000 by the third year, with overhead costs in that year expected to be $200,000 and an average net value per customer projected at $3, the company will need to develop a customer list of about 334,000 names over the initial two-year period. (This estimate is an over-simplification, since it assumes no customer acquisition cost in the third year. We have not included third-year acquisition cost because it would entail too in-depth a discussion for the purpose of this briefing.)

In a going operation, in which capital for customer acquisition is derived wholly from the business, the profit aspiration policy is based on the net gain expected from operations for each year. Assume that management wishes to show a profit of $5 million in the coming year. Profit on sales to customers, after adjusting for overhead costs, is expected to reach $6 million. This leaves $1 million for customer acquisition.

Return on Investment

When management adopts the return-on-investment policy, it establishes the return it would like to see on the cost of acquiring customers. Implicit in this approach is the concept that customer acquisition costs represent an investment in the business. The goal is expressed as a percentage of acquisition cost over time, for example, a return on investment of 100 percent over four years.

Let us say that customer acquisition and customer value data for an allotted time span point to a spin-off of $5.69 in net income per average customer. The total is divided among four years as follows: $1.84, first year; $1.50, second year; $1.25, third year; and $1.10, fourth. However, income generated two to four years hence will not have the same value it does today. Therefore, future income must be converted to current values, with the following formula:

$$V = \frac{R_1}{(1 + i)} + \frac{R_2}{(1 + i)^2} + \ldots + \frac{R_n}{(1 + i)^n}$$

where

$$
\begin{aligned}
V &= \text{Present value.} \\
R_1, R_2, \ldots, R_n &= \text{Net income from average customer in first, second, } \ldots, n\text{th year.} \\
i &= \text{Discount rate of income (the interest rate at which each year's income must be converted to the present value).}
\end{aligned}
$$

Assuming a 10 percent discount rate of income and a net income per customer of $5.69 over the four-year period, customer value would be:

$$V = \frac{1.84}{(1 + .10)} + \frac{1.50}{(1 + .10)^2} + \frac{1.25}{(1 + .10)^3} + \frac{1.10}{(1 + .10)^4} = \$4.61$$

Assuming a 100 percent ROI over four years, under these conditions customer acquisition costs cannot exceed one-half the discounted net value, or $2.31.

The declining rate of customer value in each year is predicated on an average attrition rate of 35 percent during the first year in which customers are acquired and 15 percent per year thereafter through the eighth year. These rates may be reduced with special promotions to inactive customers. The cost of acquiring customers is amortized over time, usually the average life-span of a customer. The list of customers is carried on the books of the company as an asset and is valued at the cost of acquisition.

Computing Customer Acquisition Cost

The cost of acquiring a customer is computed in the following manner.

14

$$C = \frac{S - (A + M + F + X)}{N}$$

where

- C = Average cost of acquiring one customer.
- S = Total sales revenue from the current advertising effort under review.
- A = Cost of advertising efforts that produced S.
- M = Cost of merchandise or service.
- F = Fulfillment cost (direct labor and material costs related to preparing and shipping orders).
- X = Cost of returned merchandise (at selling price), refurbishing, and repair.
- N = Number of customers acquired from the advertising effort under review.

The result is usually a negative figure, which represents the customer acquisition cost. Zero indicates that customers were acquired at breakeven (no cost), and a positive figure means that customers were acquired at a profit, also considered to be at no cost. When advertising is designed to solicit inquiries, the cost of obtaining them is part of the advertising cost.

The customer acquisition cost of each media vehicle and media type is computed separately, as it will vary for each vehicle and type. A key that identifies the source of every response is imprinted on each response vehicle (the reply card, order-form, coupon, or other means of customer response). Overhead is not included in the computation, because it varies as a percentage of sales revenue but remains fixed in terms of absolute dollars. The inclusion of overhead would prove misleading, since it might attribute the sins of poor administrative management to media performance but, of course, it has to be taken into account in a profit-and-loss statement.

Computing Customer Value

We have been alluding to customer value. How is it defined? The value of a customer is the sum total of the net profit the customer contributes during his or her life-span as a customer. The customer value in any given year is computed as follows:

$$V_1 = \frac{S + L - (A + M + F + X)}{N}$$

where

V_1 = Value of average customer in a given year.
S = Total sales revenue from customers for year.
L = Income from rental of customer list to other, noncompetitive marketers.
A = Cost of all advertising efforts directed at customers during the year (promotion packages, catalogs).
M = Cost of merchandise or service.
F = Fulfillment costs.
X = Cost of returned merchandise (at selling price) and refurbishing and repair.
N = Number of customers.

The above equation is used to compute the average value per customer for each year under review. The sum of the values of $V_1 \ldots , V_n$ represents the average customer value in terms of profit contributed over the number of years under review. Implicit in each of the three profit policies is a maximum customer acquisition cost that is directly related to customer value. Computation of customer cost and customer value over time will establish the maximum customer cost related to the chosen policy. Therefore, by combining test results and historical data in the two formulas, the marketer can project the probable customer value from customers acquired from each media vehicle tested, and can include in future media schedules only those vehicles that are likely to produce customers whose future buying pattern, on average, will meet the company's profit policy criteria (see following section and Testing).

MEDIA PLANNING AND BUDGETING

The double thrust of direct marketing is to generate sales from the house list and to acquire customers. The discussion that follows outlines the criteria for developing budgets and media plans for each.

House-List Media Planning and Budgeting

Direct mail is the medium of choice for generating sales revenue from the house list. The budget is based on the number of profitable mailings that can be made to each selected segment of the list over the budget period. Which segments to use and how often mailings should be made to each of them is the direct marketer's most important task. All, or almost all, profit is linked to that house list, and profit provides the leverage for acquiring new customers. Mailing frequency to each segment is assigned on the basis of the following customer criteria:

Recency, the date of the most recent purchase.
Frequency, the number of purchases over time.
Monetary value, the total amount spent by the customer over time and the average value of each purchase.
Payment behavior.
Source, the media through which customers were acquired.
Offer.
Product-line composition.

Recency, Frequency, and Monetary Value

Using six-month periods as a base, selection of segments is made on the basis of the most recent and most frequent activity and the highest monetary value. "Highest" and "most" are relevant terms. Each is interpreted in terms of customer activity experienced by each individual operation. Those with the "best" activity constitute the prime segment and are solicited most frequently — as often as 22 times a year. The frequency of mailings to each segment declines progressively in relation to its profitability.

One company, for example, reported some years ago that customers who made two or more purchases (frequency) within the latest six-month period (recency) for a total of $20 (monetary value) made up its prime segment at that time. Those who made one purchase within the latest six-month to 12-month period for a total of $2 represented its poorest segment.

Segments are selected from the inactive and former customer groups based on the same recency, frequency, and monetary value criteria, using six-month periods as a base. Mailings to each segment are also made less and less frequently. Segments are eliminated from mailings when response becomes unprofitable. Inquirer segments are selected on the basis of recency only.

Payment Behavior

Data on payment behavior helps identify customers who are having difficulty meeting current obligations, which indicates an inability to make new purchases. Hence, fewer mailings should be directed to them, even if they meet the recency, frequency, and monetary value criteria.

Source

Purchasing activity is related to the media type through which the customer was acquired. Customers acquired through direct mail are more responsive as a group than are those picked up through other media in the following *descending* order: magazine, newspaper, TV, radio, and all others. (Existing customers submit names of friends and relatives, who become customers. Such names are called *referrals*, and their submission is a *source*.)

Offer

The nature of the offer used to acquire customers affects future buying behavior. A group acquired through a free-gift offer, for example, will respond at a lower rate, unless a similar type of offer is made in house-list mailings. Conversely, if the acquisition offer provides no incentive other than that inherent in the product, future solicitations will result in a higher level of response. The acquisition offer should be carefully examined in relation to its effect on future customer activity.

Product-Line Composition

The number of products in the line and how their sale is promoted affect mailing frequency. Twelve products sold through individual product offerings would require a dozen mailings, one for each product. A catalog that advertises all 12 would require only one mailing.

Media Planning and Budgeting for Customer Acquisition

Media planning and budgeting for the acquisition of new customers is governed by the profit policy established by management. The direct marketer's chief task in developing a customer acquisition program is to determine which media vehicles produce customers at a cost and with a value within constraints of the policy. For example, management adopts the return-on-investment policy and sets its goal as 100 percent ROI over four years. Policy constraints would dictate that the marketer invest only in a mix of those media vehicles that acquire customers at an average cost-to-value ratio of 1:2. To achieve that cost-to-value ratio will require the use of certain techniques that help reduce the cost of customers while increasing profit, such as media selection, support media, market segmentation, cost/time trade-offs, and seasonal variations.

18

Media Selection

All media types or vehicles have a different response behavior pattern, just as their cost per thousand (cpm) varies. All the general marketer needs to know is that his or her ad appears in a media vehicle that reaches the heavy user segment of the market. But the direct marketer needs more. The direct marketer must identify those media vehicles that have a high incidence of readers with a propensity to buy by mail.

In the absence of performance data on various media vehicles, selection may be based on a study of a representative sample of recent issues of publications whose audience characteristics and editorial content fit the product or service. The study will encompass three factors: (1) presence of an editorial feature aimed at mail-order buyers, for instance, a shopper's guide, (2) percentage of total advertising space devoted to direct marketing ads, and (3) percentage of space used by sellers of competitive or related products or services. Each of these factors can be quantified and converted to an index that will help the marketer select those media vehicles that should be tested. Those that have the high index number are the most likely to perform within the allowable cost per customer (cpc) limits.

Support Media

A second media type used in conjunction with the vehicle that carries the burden of getting orders will increase response. The main thrust of the support ads is to develop interest in the offer carried in the other media type. Typically, local spots on TV and radio are used to support newspaper and direct mail campaigns. We were involved in one case in which response to newspaper preprinted inserts was increased by 95 percent with a TV budget equal to 15 percent of the print budget.

Generally, attempts to support magazine insertions (except newspaper magazine supplements) with broadcast media do not work to advantage because of the relatively low level of market penetration of magazines within limited geographic areas. To be economical, support should be limited to campaigns that reach a high percentage of a total market area. The amount budgeted for this purpose in each market is a percentage of either the print, or direct mail budgets, or both, in each market area. The percentage depends on the additional orders that will be generated by support. We have found that an allotment of 10 to 20 percent of the print-media budget within each market area is about the most productive relationship. The support technique should be tested in one group of markets (at least five) against no support in another group of demographically matched markets to help determine whether it will increase response to specific campaigns, and by how much.

Market Segmentation

Market segmentation is an absolute necessity in direct marketing. In this context, the major difference between general and direct marketing stems from the fact that direct marketing must pick up sufficient orders from each media vehicle to meet the customer cost/value criteria. Segmentation is the product of a market profile made up of demographic and psychographic characteristics. Demographic data include such information as disposable income, discretionary spending power, number and age of children, education, age, year and make of car(s) owned, occupational class. Psychographic data can usually be extrapolated from the special-interest content of a magazine and, for direct mail lists, from the type of products purchased.

The average unit of sale is also important. It is usually reported in descriptions of mail-order lists and can be extrapolated from prices of goods or services offered in magazine advertising of related or competitive products. The importance of the average unit of sale lies in the fact that marketers can usually get a handle on the relationship between the price paid for one type of product and the price level of their own product line. For example, a marketer knows that a woman who pays $10 for a hat is not likely to spend $75 for a pair of shoes. Similarly, a magazine with a high incidence of ads offering low-end merchandise is not likely to perform well for higher-priced merchandise offers.

Certain general-interest magazines offer demographic and geographic selections based on readership studies. One prominent national affairs magazine offers a selection of 174 editions. One edition, for example, reaches 1.2 million subscribers with an average income of $27,000. Another edition goes to an even more select group — some 300,000 company presidents, corporate officers, partners, and directors of firms. Psychographic selection is

inherent in special-interest magazines by the nature of the editorial content.

The programming for every radio station is designed to reach a specific class of listener — teenagers with rock music, adults with drive-time news, and ethnic groups with foreign language broadcasts. Television emphasizes the demographic composition of its audience in its attempts to lure advertisers. Programs are designed to reach a specific class of audience. One program, for example, may be considered the best for attracting women in the 18 to 34-year-old age group; another as the best regular program for reaching an audience 50 years of age and over; and a third as effective in reaching a larger audience of children (ages 2 to 11). In direct mail, market segmentation is achieved through the selection of lists made up of populations that meet predetermined socioeconomic criteria. Direct mail is the most effective market segmentation tool available, whether used for advertising or for direct marketing.

Time/Cost Trade-off

The relationship between cost and the number of customers that has to be acquired within a fixed time frame influences the selection of media types and vehicles. For example, a multipage preprinted newspaper insert acquires three customers for every customer acquired by a full-page black-and-white run-of-paper (ROP) newspaper ad. But the insert costs four times as much. Even with the higher cost, the preprinted insert may be the medium of choice if the marketer needs to build up the house list within a brief time frame, and if the cost per customer does not exceed pre-established limits. Sometimes it is preferable to pay more for a customer in order to accelerate growth. A larger house list offers an opportunity to take advantage of economies of scale and to increase profit.

Seasonal Variations

Whether a given promotional effort is used to acquire new customers or to generate repeat sales from customers, its effectiveness is influenced by seasonal factors. The best time to advertise varies among industries and companies. This means that marketers have to determine their own seasonal indices through testing. If no company experience is available, the following indices, developed by *World Book*, will serve until you develop your own:

Month	Index
January	124
February	120
March	88
April	89
May	89
June	83
July	91
August	108
September	98
October	112
November	100
December	98

These indices are based on data derived from direct mail, much of which uses third-class, bulk-rate mail service to practically every region in the country. They reflect delays between delivery of mail to the post office of origin and delivery to prospective customers. Indices based on other types of media may differ in some respects. Bob Stone believes that these indices coincide with the experience of most mass mailers.[1] Our own testing program over a three-year period confirms the findings.

THE OFFER

An offer is a proposition made to the prospect as an inducement to respond. It can take the form of a special price, an outstanding product benefit, a sweepstakes or other type of contest, an incentive premium, or a free trial. The offer must be powerful enough to create an instant, positive, buying decision. Above all, it must be uncomplicated. Complex offers lead to misunderstandings, loss of interest, suspicion, or a combination of all three, each of which reduces response and, therefore, effectiveness.

Another aspect of the offer is that it tends to position a product or company. It is therefore essential to design an offer related to the desired market position. Don't surround the product line or

company with an offer that suggests a "bargain basement" image, when the aim is to position both with a high-quality image. The offer used to acquire customers will have an impact on their future buying habits, so let the marketer beware. Customers acquired through incentive premiums, for example, will not generate as much repeat business as others unless incentives are offered in future solicitations. Here is a sampling of popular types of offers.

Incentive Premiums

Offers that incorporate incentive premiums, known as free keepers, tend to increase response significantly. They are offered as rewards for trying the product with the understanding that buyers may keep the premium should they elect to return the product for refund or credit. The most effective premiums, from the standpoint of acquiring customers with a higher value, are those that have a close kinship to the product(s) or service(s) offered for sale. Certainly they must have a strong appeal to the market segment being solicited. Tickets to the Super Bowl are not likely to create a high level of interest among prospects for classical records, for example.

The most important factor in selecting an incentive premium is its "fit" to the product or service being offered. Its perceived value by the customer should be related to the price of the primary item. Premiums should not be selected on the basis of their cost as a pre-established percentage of sale. Keep in mind that the cost of the promotion is static and that the cost per order is a variable related to the number and dollar value of orders received. The function of the incentive, therefore, is to reduce this variable and, at the same time, liquidate its own cost. When testing various incentive premiums, it is wise to study results on the basis of their impact on the cost per order and on the effect such offers have on future sales to acquired customers.

Price Offers

Price can also serve as an offer. While it is a delicate matter in any form of marketing, it takes on added significance in direct marketing, because the prospects do not have the opportunity to see a live demonstration of the product under circumstances that allow them to compare prices of competing brands. A price that is too low for a product that is being described as highest quality loses credibility. Nor should a price be placed sharply below the level to which people are accustomed, unless it represents liquidation of the manufacturer's stock, last season's model, an introductory offer, and similar cogent reasons.

Payment Terms

Payment terms can be used to relieve anxiety among people who are wary of buying sight unseen. Credit is more effective than COD or cash with order, and a money-back guarantee, with cash or credit, is a must. Monthly payment terms on items above a certain price level tend to boost response. In a continuity program, payment for each item within 30 days after receipt has proved effective. In such cases, the offer should include the privilege of refusing any one of the items in the series or of canceling at any point in the program.

One unique anxiety-relieving money-back guarantee is that used by a Utah marketer who offers a formula for getting rich in real estate. He promises to hold a respondent's check for 30 days before presenting it for payment. He then goes one step further and says that any respondent who doesn't trust him to hold the check may postdate it by 30 days.

Free-Trial Periods

Free-trial offers have become routine in direct marketing. They are an effective technique, the ultimate weapon in relieving consumer anxiety. On the other hand, they can increase the seller's anxiety, since some people will keep products and refuse to pay on the assumption that no action will be taken against them. Companies can protect themselves against such losses by using routine credit-checking procedures prior to shipment and, where possible, by confining offers to market segments for which the demographic profile indicates a high degree of family stability. Products or services that have no value unless payment is received, such as insurance policies, add to selling costs, because they require a conversion series to consummate the sale. The expenses of the series are part of the cost per order.

Deadline Date

Two types of deadline-date offer are popular. In one type, the prospect is offered a reward, such as an incentive premium, for responding by a deadline date. In the other, orders received beyond the deadline date are rejected. In addition to increasing sales, both offers speed up the flow of orders. The deadline-date offer helps push the mildly interested group toward a positive buying decision. It is frequently associated with sweepstakes and contests in which a special bonus prize is offered to one or more people who respond by an established date that precedes the date by which all entries must be received. Response to deadline-date offers tends to be better with a shorter exposure time between the message and the deadline date. This period is influenced by the media type used, as each has a different life-span.

Negative Option

The negative option offer gives the customer an opportunity to reject an offer — to exercise a negative option — by a specified date, after which the product will be shipped. Book clubs use the negative option offer. This type of offer can be used only after a customer has been acquired and has agreed to the terms. Otherwise, it is illegal.

Unless prohibited by law, an unconditional money-back guarantee should accompany all types of offers. These are only a handful of the many different types of offers that can be made. One magazine article[2] has identified as many as 99.

ADVERTISING COPY: GENERAL vs. DIRECT MARKETING

The mission of advertising in direct marketing is to motivate the prospect to place an order NOW. It must get the consumer to respond affirmatively with a single exposure in a matter of minutes. Cumulative effect, recall, and other measures of advertising effectiveness have no place in the direct marketer's lexicon. The only thing that counts is the number of orders generated by each individual ad. Consequently, advertising copy is written differently for general and direct marketing. The primary difference between them stems from the principle that exposure to advertising is a passive learning experience.

The thrust of general advertising is to demand attention, get readership and, through it, create a high level of awareness, identification, and remembrance of the product for action at a later time. Headline words and phrases for general print advertising are therefore selected more for their attention-getting prowess than for their ability to create an immediate-purchase-decision climate. In contrast, direct marketing copy must turn passivity into immediate action. It has to (1) entice the reader to voluntarily interrupt the activity in which he or she is engaged, (2) create an immediate-purchase-decision climate, and (3) make the sale.

The general principles of copywriting discussed in this section are based on the differences between general and direct marketing advertising. They are intended as a guide to the marketing manager, whose function is to outline objectives to the copywriter and pass judgment on what has been written.

• *Make the copy length suit the need.* One rule generally applied to the length of copy is that it should be long enough to cover the subject, but short enough to maintain the reader's interest. Direct mail letters and print-media ads made up of 1,000 words or more of text are not uncommon. The amount of information and persuasion required by each prospect varies with the level of interest in the product or service — high interest, medium interest, no interest. Some readers will go through all of the copy before making a buying decision. Others will read only the first two or three paragraphs. But a decision to stop reading does not necessarily mean a loss of interest. It can also mean that a positive buying decision has been made. The need for lengthy copy is not a license to pad or to write drivel; it is a function of keeping the audience interested.

• *Aim headline at high- and medium-interest levels.* Headlines serve as a market segmentation device. Many copywriters foolishly try to write headlines that appeal to the total universe, an impossible task even in media that reach a specific special-interest group. Headline copy is more effective when it is geared toward the high- and medium-interest audience. It is better to attract these two groups, which will represent the bulk of sales, than to risk losing them in an attempt to reach everybody.

Moreover, even the most specialized media attract readers with varying levels of interest in the subject matter and with different discretionary spending power. A publication devoted to electronic reproduction of music, for example, will have among its readership many people who would like to have the performance of a $5,000 piece of equipment, but only a few who can actually afford it. The headline should be aimed at the few, for they are the ones who are most likely to buy. The balance of the audience may read the ad, but will not respond with an order. That is why studies that show a high level of "noted," "recalled," and other reader responses can mislead the general marketer into believing that

26

certain ads are effective. This is not the case with the direct marketer, who measures advertising effectiveness in terms of orders received and customers acquired.

Don't use words or phrases in headlines on the attention-getting factor alone. State the benefit or offer in straightforward copy without trying to be cute. Here are two examples of this technique:

"How to Wake Up the Financial Genius in You"
"One of These $77,000 Dream Houses Will Be Awarded to Our Next Grand Prize Winners"

The first, used in space advertising, states a benefit. The copy goes on to offer a formula for getting rich in real estate. The other, used on the envelope of a direct mail package, stresses the offer, a sweepstakes. It is aimed at getting subscriptions for a home decorating magazine.

• *Sell the premium first.* The magazine offer mentioned earlier helps point up the importance of selling the premium first. It also demonstrates how a premium related to the product helps sell the product and qualify the prospect. In this case, the person interested in a "dream house," whether he or she expects to win, has a strong interest in his or her home — the most likely type of person to read the magazine and the very person the magazine's advertisers want to reach.

• *Position the product.* Position the product before you begin to write. A tool offer, for example, can be positioned against either the do-it-yourself or the professional market. If the former is desired, copy that emphasizes benefits to the homeowner is required: "Now, get professional results every time on all those little odd jobs around the house with the new, revolutionary widget." Positioning the product against the professional market calls for changing the emphasis to business benefits: "The New BMT-47 Widget increases profits by 25 percent, cuts on-the-job time by 40 percent, reduces call-backs by 95 percent, gives you a big edge over your competitors."

• *Ask for order early and frequently.* The first request for an order should come within the first four paragraphs, and should be repeated at least two times in the text, and once at the close. The request should always be accompanied by instructions on how to place an order; a benefit from making the purchase or the conditions of sale, or both, should also accompany the request.

• *Don't distract attention.* Copy should hardly ever invite the reader to see details in another piece of the mailing or section of the ad. For cases in which certain information cannot be handled in the body of the letter or ad (for example, insurance rate tables), extend the invitation as late in the copy as possible. References in one piece to more information in another distract attention, even if the reader does not look for the other piece right away. Such references make the reader wonder what he or she is going to find. It is therefore better to tell readers what you want them to know while you have their attention. The corollary is that the letter and brochure of a direct mail package should each stand on its own in making the sale.

• *Entice the reader to continue reading.* Entice the reader to turn the page or continue to the next column by continuing a thought: "You'll never again have to . . ." is an example of this technique. It leaves the reader in midthought. The use of connective phrases at the end of a paragraph is also effective: "But that's not all . . ." "And, also consider this . . . ."

• *Back up benefit claims.* Benefit claims should be backed up with testimonials from customers. Testimonials can be obtained by including a form in the fulfillment package for customers to fill in.

• *Relieve anxieties of the prospect.* Anxiety-relieving devices, such as an unqualified money-back guarantee, help allay the reader's doubts.

• *Make positive statements.* Don't remind the reader about inflation, crime in the streets, and other socioeconomic problems. If you have to, don't put the prospect in the negative situation. Instead, point out how the product helps the prospective customer avoid the negative situation.

• *Emphasize benefits.* Describe the product or service in text copy in terms of how it will benefit the reader. Prospects are more interested in how a watch will help them get places on time than they are in knowing how it is made and how great the company is that made it.

• *Don't put down competing products.* Call attention to a good feature of the competing product that is also available in yours. Then mention another characteristic of yours that is not present in the competition's product, and explain why this makes your product last longer, look better, function more efficiently. The bottom line is that competing products are good, but yours is better.

• *Be believable.* Don't make unbelievable claims, even if they're true. If you must use them, label them as such and prove their veracity with factual information or testimonials from identifiable people.

• *Accept prospect's attitude.* Accept the prospect's attitude as it is, not as you would like it to be. First get their acceptance. Then take them where you want them to go.

• *Avoid arguments.* Don't be contentious. You'll lose all arguments, because the reader can turn the page or toss your message into the waste basket.

• *Think about meanings of words.* Don't consider just one meaning of a word but all meanings and connotations. "Integrated" is a fine word to describe circuits but it may raise other, distracting thoughts among people whose first encounter with the word revolves around what the Supreme Court said in Brown vs. Board of Education. Such words, when properly used, do not convey the wrong meaning. Rather, they remind people of another experience (pleasant or distasteful) and cause the mind to wander from your message. Avoid their use wherever possible.

• *Use the perpendicular pronoun.* Wherever it fits, use the word "I." There are situations when it is effective to establish a "you-and-I" relationship with the prospect, for instance, an "I" experience that was enjoyed by use of a product or service. "*I* got rich using the service now available to *you*," "If *I* were sitting at your dining room table with *you* right now, you would probably ask *me* . . . " are examples of this technique.

• *Involve the prospect.* Copy should help involve the prospect emotionally and mentally. For example, copy that invites prospective customers to join the copywriter on a sightseeing trip in Rome can evoke mental pictures of the sights and sounds and move them emotionally. Questions can sometimes involve the prospect mentally: "What would you do if . . . ?"

• *Create social acceptability.* Copy should make the point that owning the product or service is socially acceptable in the prospect's socioeconomic class. "Thousands of people already own . . ." and "Some of your neighbors on Clancy Street are enjoying . . ." are examples of this technique. The opposite is also true in some applications. When making an offer to a group whose psycho-graphics indicate that they like to set the pace, it is better to use the "be-the-first-on-your-block" approach.

TESTING

The goals of testing in direct marketing are similar to those of general marketing. However, direct marketing places greater emphasis on objective data, since it is more easily measured. The direct marketer is not encumbered by the intervention of third parties, such as dealers, distributors, and sales persons, who may skew test results. The direct marketer has complete control over each variable being tested.

A standard testing device is the A/B split. Using this technique, the direct marketer may test a situation in which two or more stimuli or variables are tested against each other in the same media vehicle. Ad A may carry one headline and ad B another. This testing device is also referred to as a two-way split. When three stimuli are tested against each other, the technique is referred to as an A/B/C split or a three-way split, and when four stimuli are used the technique is called the A/B/C/D split, and so on.

The direct marketer can use A/B splits in almost all media so efficiently that a different offer can be delivered to every other household in one neighborhood, or even to every third or fourth household if desirable. In a perfect two-way split, for example, exposure to the A side stimulus is limited to the first, third, fifth, and seventh households receiving the media vehicle, while the B side goes to the second, fourth, sixth, and eighth households. Other possibilities include a perfect A/B/C split in which exposure A is limited to the first, fourth, seventh, and tenth households; B to the second, fifth, eighth, and eleventh households; and C to the third, sixth, ninth, and twelfth households.

The test is controlled not only through such techniques as the A/B split, but also by the very nature of direct marketing which enables the customer to respond directly to the advertiser. The direct response enables the marketer to apply statistical techniques to actual numbers, that is, to objective data that shows the precise number of people who took the action requested. Because that action results from clearly identifiable stimuli represented by the variables, the direct marketer can adopt the most effective

30

stimuli with a degree of confidence not experienced by the general marketer. Furthermore, because such data is available much faster than through general marketing techniques, favorable market opportunities can continue to be exploited while they still exist. These advantages are available to the direct marketer who is willing to adhere to certain rules and to the strict discipline required in structuring and conducting tests. The direct marketer, like the general marketer, is involved in test marketing and market testing. The lexicon and emphasis may be different, but the objectives are the same.

Market Testing

In direct maketing, market testing is media testing. To again quote Frank Vos, "The medium is the market." The purpose of market testing in direct marketing is to determine which of the available media vehicles produce orders (acquire customers) at a cost commensurate with the cost/value criteria. Testing should be conducted by using the offer, copy, and other elements that have a track record of success in other media. This rule can be violated when the medium being tested represents a new market segment for which there is good reason to believe that a different offer or copy approach, tailored to the market, will prove more productive. In such instances, the new variable should be tested against the successful one, which serves as the control.

Marketers frequently overlook opportunities to broaden the market, either because they have preconceived notions about the market composition or because they have had success with a particular market segment. Both lines of reasoning should be challenged by testing media vehicles that reach market segments whose profiles go beyond the spectrum of their experience.

Size of Test. The minimum number of responses required for effective statistical evaluation determines the number of exposures needed to test each media vehicle. Unfortunately, there is no adequate statistical method for arriving at the number of exposures. The equation commonly used to determine sample size ($n = S^2pq/L^2$) is *not* applicable to a direct marketing situation because it assumes that a universe is homogeneous or that a random sample of a universe is available. Neither assumption is true for any media vehicle. However, this obstacle can be side-stepped by employing the five-way-split technique described under Media Testing Capabilities.

Our experience has shown that direct mail lists can be tested adequately with 5,000 names, magazine ads and newspaper pre-printed inserts with a circulation of 50,000, and newspaper ads with a circulation of 100,000. As a practical consideration, the size of the test will, in many cases, be governed by the smallest circulation a media vehicle is willing to sell.

Test Marketing

In direct marketing, test marketing is more frequently used to try out offers, prices, copy, graphics, and other stimuli than to test new products. Its purpose is to develop a breakthrough, to find a stimulus that will *significantly* increase response. There are certain general rules to be followed in conducting tests of this type:

1. Clearly define the stimulus to be tested and exercise the discipline necessary to adhere to the definition. Don't allow extraneous elements to be introduced.
2. Be certain that the test results will provide meaningful data that can be used profitably. Do not test trivia or elements intended to satisfy someone's curiosity.
3. Introduce only one variable in each test package or ad, whether it be price, copy platform, or headline.
4. Test against a control, using the same quantity of names or the same circulation base on all sides of the test. The control and all test ads must break on the same day.
5. Use at least five media vehicles in each media type. This provides a test of consistency and a test of significance of difference (see Analysis of Test Results). Each vehicle carries all sides or panels of the test and uses A/B split techniques.
6. As discussed under Market Testing, the number of exposures should be great enough to provide sufficient responses for statistical evaluation. The criterion is to obtain as many exposures on each side of a test as can provide at least 50 responses from each. Hence, if the expected response from newspapers is 1 percent, an A/B split should be run in newspapers with a circulation of at least 100,000.

Testing is a continuous activity. Market testing should be conducted to broaden the market, and is frequently combined with test marketing to improve response. Tests should be conducted while current efforts are going well, because of the time lag from conception of a new approach, execution of the test, and subsequent rollout. The marketer who doesn't take action until response levels begin to show decline loses valuable time in retrenching.

Media Testing Capabilities

A firm base in the way in which media can be used for testing will help marketers structure tests to meet the criteria outlined in this section.

Direct Mail

Lists used in direct mail can be divided into as many segments as necessary to meet the criteria of the testing situation. In a market (list) test in which five separate groups are needed to adjust for the lack of homogeneity and randomness, 5,000 names are divided into groups of 1,000 each without disturbing the sequence in which they are supplied. Each group is assigned a different key number.

The number of splits for a test marketing program in direct mail is limited only by the number of names available and the budget. For example, if the plan calls for testing six different offers, break up the list into six segments on an nth-name basis. Assign a different key to each segment. Never test by using one variable on one list and another on a second list, because response patterns will differ from list to list, making the results invalid. Wherever possible, use names from the house list for test marketing.

Newspapers

Newspapers represent seven different media vehicles: Daily ROP, Sunday ROP, Sunday magazine supplements, Sunday and/or daily preprinted advertising inserts, Sunday TV supplements, and Sunday comics. Each has a different cpm and response behavior pattern.

Each of these media, with the exception of preprints, offers only A/B splits. The number of splits available in preprints is limited by the printer's press capabilities. The greatest number of splits the authors are familiar with is five. In a five-way-split test, for example, every fifth copy carries either a different message or key number, or both. The preprints are collated and delivered to newspapers in the sequence in which they come off the press, thus eliminating the danger of clustering one message in one block or other geographic section.

A multisplit test marketing program can be conducted in the other newspaper media vehicles by running two-way splits in as many matching markets as there are panels in the test. The "control" ad is run in each market against a different test ad. Care in selecting matching markets will increase the validity of results.

Magazines

Multisplits for market testing in magazines are available only when bind-ins, also called tip-ins, are used. The procedure is the same as that used for newspaper preprints. Multisplits for test marketing in run-of-book (ROB) ads can be accomplished by using regional editions in the same way as described for newspapers. The number of splits is limited by the number of regional editions available.

Broadcasting

Market testing programs in broadcasting are conducted on the basis of TV program and radio station programming formats. TV ads should be run with programs that attract the desired market segment and radio ads on stations whose format reaches the target group. Use five radio stations with the same format in separate markets and five TV stations in separate markets with ads scheduled to run with the same (or similar) programs in each market area. Test marketing programs in broadcasting are more difficult to conduct, since there is really no effective means of getting an A/B split in a market. However, running each side of the test in a series of markets on matched stations has provided a fair amount of validity in some test marketing programs. Our own inclination is to adapt the winning stimulus from tests in other media types to broadcasting.

ANALYSIS OF TEST RESULTS

The precision with which response data to direct marketing efforts can be measured will be welcomed by marketers who wrestle with marketing and advertising research results in other forms of marketing. Very few questions are left unanswered after a test has been carried out, because it gives the researcher hard data on which to base conclusions. Every analysis of test results begins with counting the number of orders received and identifying their source and the stimuli responsible for them, assuming, of course, that the data comes from tests that were properly structured and conducted.

Analysis of market testing data involves the use of different statistical methods from those used to analyze test marketing response. The objective in market testing is to determine which media type or vehicle can consistently produce orders (or customers) at, or below, the established cost criterion. The primary goal of test marketing analysis is to determine whether differences in response to various stimuli are significant or the result of chance, and whether the conclusions are reliable.

Market Testing Analysis

By merely counting the number of orders and dollars received from a test ad, subtracting the costs, and dividing the difference by the number of orders, we arrive at the cost per order. The cost is either above or below the affordable limits. If the cost per order is affordable, we then move from the test sample to the total circulation of those media vehicles that have produced sufficient orders to meet the customer cost criterion.

This may appear simple and straightforward; however, we cannot assume that the level of response from the total circulation of each media vehicle will be precisely equal to that of the test, since there is always the possibility of having a poor sample or the results of a chance variation. These factors can be adjusted for with the following technique.

Dividing the total test quantity into five segments as outlined earlier measures the homogeneity of the "universe" — the media vehicle readers — being tested. No universe of this type is homogeneous, but some are more homogeneous than others. Say a test of 50,000 preprinted inserts in the Podunk Journal generates 185 orders, .37 percent. The response from each segment of 10,000 is shown in Table 1. The response from another 50,000 inserts in the Keokuk Review is also .37 percent, and that from each segment is also indicated in Table 1. Note the wide variation in response from each segment of the Podunk Journal, particularly the skew in segment 4. The response to the Keokuk Review is almost evenly divided among the five segments.

In the absence of five separate observations, we would be misled into projecting the same response from each newspaper in a rollout,* because we would have only the overall average (.37 percent) on which to base the projection. Projections made on the basis of five observations for each media vehicle will show, however, that the rollout response from the *Podunk Journal* will deviate significantly from the test, but not from a rollout in the *Keokuk Review*.

Table 1. Comparison of response from tests of preprinted inserts in two publications

Segment	Quantity	Response Number	%
Podunk Journal Response			
1	10,000	36	.36
2	10,000	22	.22
3	10,000	21	.21
4	10,000	74	.74
5	10,000	32	.32
	50,000	185	.37
Keokuk Review Response			
1	10,000	33	.33
2	10,000	38	.38
3	10,000	40	.40
4	10,000	36	.36
5	10,000	38	.38
	50,000	185	.37

The following equation can be an effective tool for measuring the degree of homogeneity in a universe and for projecting rollout response levels when a five-way split is used:

$$S = \sqrt{\frac{\Sigma d^2}{n}}$$

where

S = Standard deviation
d^2 = Sum of square of deviations
n = Number of observations

*The process of shifting from a test sample to total circulation.

Let us apply the equation to the data for the *Podunk Journal,* as shown in Table 1.

Segment	% Response	d^b	d^2
1	.36	.01	.0001
2	.22	.15	.0225
3	.21	.16	.0256
4	.74	− .37	.1369
5	.32	.05	.0025
	.37		.1876

[a] Mean response.
[b] Deviation from mean.

Thus,

$$S = \sqrt{\frac{.1876}{5}} = .19\%$$

Hence, the chances are 68 out of 100 (68 percent level of confidence) that response to a rollout in the *Podunk Journal* will probably fall somewhere between .18 percent and .56 percent (.37 percent $\pm$ .19 percent). When the formula is applied to the data on the *Keokuk Review* shown in Table 1, you get a value of .023 for *S,* which projects a response range of .35 to .39 percent to a rollout in that publication. Experience shows that rollout response usually moves toward the low end of the predicted range. Hence, rollouts should be confined to those media vehicles whose predicted lowest possible response lies within the established customer cost criterion.

Experts in sampling analysis may question the validity of this equation for projecting rollout response on a purely theoretical level. But it has proved very efficient in our experience, when applied to market testing data. In fact, the equation that is commonly recommended,

$$Gp = \sqrt{pq/n}$$

does not work as well as the above equation in that it fails to take into account the possibility of a poor sample.

Test Marketing Analysis

The purpose of test marketing is to determine which of the stimuli tested will be most productive. Four statistical tests are applied to the raw response data in order to arrive at the most likely conclusion: arithmetic average, modified average, consistency, and significance.

The test of arithmetic average (or mean) compares the average response to each side of the test. The total of all responses generated by all media vehicles on each side of the test is averaged (percentage response and dollar value) and compared. The variable having either the highest percentage of response or dollar value, or both, is assumed to be the most productive.

The test of modified average is used to eliminate distortion to which extreme values may subject the arithmetic average. In this test, all extreme values—those response levels that deviate significantly from the others — are eliminated, and a new arithmetic average (modified average) is computed. The extreme values, attributable either to unusual competitive or other activities in a given market, or to error in transmission, recording, or processing of raw data, can be eliminated if attempts to discover the reasons for their presence fail, or if they cannot be adjusted. They may also be discarded when found to be caused by unusual market conditions.

The test of consistency is used to determine the reliability of the test of arithmetic average. It shows whether the variable that performed best on the basis of average response is likely to do so consistently. Assuming an A/B split in each of five media vehicles, a total of ten observations is available, five for each side of the test.

Prepare a table that shows the percentage response from each of the five vehicles. Then count the number of times that one side performed better than the other, to determine whether it is likely to do so consistently over time. If one stimulus performs better than the other, five times out of five (100 percent consistency), you can be fairly certain that it will do so consistently in the future. The test of consistency will confirm the test of arithmetic average.

The test of significance of difference in mean response gives a good indication of whether the differences in response to each side of the test are the result of the difference in stimuli or of chance. Whether the differences are statistically significant can be tested by such methods as the chi-square test.

When data derived from test marketing efforts pass these four tests, the direct marketer can make a rollout decision with a high degree of confidence. Indeed, the degree of confidence can be quantified. All projections must be adjusted for seasonal variations in response.

FULFILLMENT

Fulfillment describes all those activities required to effect the delivery of products or services to buyers. A good fulfillment system will go unnoticed, a bad one can totally destroy an otherwise efficient marketing operation. Fulfillment comprises the following functions:

Design of ordering procedures
Design of order forms
Receipt and recording of orders
Processing of orders
Credit checking
Inventory control
Billing
Shipping
Complaint processing
Handling returned merchandise
Security

Each of these activities is designed to achieve one major objective: Keep the customer happy. Undelivered merchandise, poor handling of returned merchandise, and other types of complaints not only lose customers for the company responsible for the problems, but create negative attitudes toward all companies that use direct marketing methods.

A Case Study

Top management's attitude toward fulfillment has a strong influence over the people who are responsible for the various activities. If, for example, top management views returned merchandise as a nuisance to be resisted, so will the fulfillment manager and the people under him or her. Here is a case drawn from our own experience, which will illustrate the point.

In the course of examining the various operations of one company, we came across a mound of returned merchandise — valuable watches, small appliances, TV sets, radios, toys, and so forth. It was explained that the merchandise was being held pending the resolution of complaints from customers. The records of the inexperienced youth in charge of the operation showed that he was engaged in long, drawn-out correspondence with irate customers — correspondence that was downright argumentative. He was proud of the job he was performing because the president of the company appreciated his resistance to replacing merchandise or refunding money — despite an unconditional money-back guarantee.

No discretion was used. All returns and complaints, regardless of the value of the merchandise, served as a signal to launch a long and expensive correspondence with the customer who, by now, was a former customer, although nobody knew it. We made the following points to the president.

1. It costs $12.50 to acquire a customer.
2. Each new customer contributed $20 to the company's profit over a five-year life-span, bringing the cost of a lost customer to $32.50.
3. The cost of replacement and refunds averaged about $10.
4. The cost of prolonged correspondence, which averaged $13.75 per return, exceeded the average cost of replacement or refund.
5. The valuable warehouse space (about 7,000 cubic feet), used to store returned goods pending resolution of disputes, could be put to better use by returning faulty merchandise to manufacturers or sending it to local repair services for refurbishing and returning salable merchandise to inventory.
6. The staff could be cut and thousands of dollars saved each year if a more liberal policy were adopted.

The president promptly changed his attitude and policy.

Fulfillment is the responsibility of the top management. Those engaged in direct marketing are fortunate in this respect, because customers are conditioned to complain in writing. Top management should read a random sample of these complaints and take appropriate action to correct inefficiencies.

The fulfillment manager should report to the marketing manager, who is responsible for acquiring new customers and keeping them active. With a poor fulfillment system, even the most brilliantly conceived marketing program will not work well. It is only fair, therefore, that the person responsible for creating profit from customers have control over how those customers are treated.

Fulfillment systems vary with each operation and are extremely complex. Any attempt to describe them within the space limitations of this briefing would probably prove misleading, but if you are interested in learning more about this subject, we recommend Stanley J. Fenvessy's article, "Importance of fulfillment in Keeping Customers Happy."[3]

2

Direct Mail

AS has already been pointed out, direct mail is one of the media types available to direct marketers. Most of the material discussed in Section 1 regarding other media types is applicable to direct mail. However, direct mail is unique in a number of ways. The major differences between direct mail and other media center on the selection and use of lists.

There are two basic types of lists: *prospect* and *house*. The prospect list, like the other media types, is used to acquire "customers," whereas the house list is used to generate profit through repeat sales. In this section, we outline methods that have proved efficient in the selection and use of prospect lists, the differences between compiled and mail-order lists, catalog preparation, package inserts, co-op, syndication, selection by duplication, and other means of cutting costs and maximizing profits in the use of direct mail.

PROSPECT LISTS

Prospect lists are the media vehicles of direct mail. They fall into two general classifications: compiled and mail order (response).

Compiled Lists

A compiled list consists of names and addresses (or addresses only) that represent six broad market categories:

1. Consumer households
2. Commercial and industrial establishments
3. Volunteer organizations
4. Professional disciplines
5. Educational
6. Government

Consumer household lists are compiled from telephone directory listings, automobile registrations, and field canvassing, and are merged into one master list, referred to as the *consumer file*. Other compilations available are names of new parents (*Family Index*) and new occupants at an address (compiled from new telephone listings).

Commercial and industrial lists are compiled from Dun & Bradstreet, trade association directories, telephone yellow pages, and other published listings. The total business and industrial universe is divided into subgroups by type of business or industry.

Lists of volunteer organizations consist of names of officers or of the organization only. All types of organizations are available, such as civic, business, professional, veteran, women, and alumni. Each represents a subgroup.

All categories of professional disciplines are compiled from directories, membership rosters, and licensing authorities. Most disciplines are subdivided according to specialty (for example, engineers are listed under such subdivisions as agricultural and chemical engineers).

The educational group comprises separate compilations of school board members, school administrators, teachers, principals, deans, and high school and college students by major area of study (for example, medical students). Lists of student names, along with college or home address, are available and, in the latter case, can be addressed to "the parents of."

Compilations of government officials are available by political subdivision and departmental responsibility, for example, law enforcement, planning, and purchasing. Members of Congress and state legislative bodies are also available.

Mail-Order Lists

Mail-order lists are made up of the same consumer households, professionals, business establishments, and so forth, found on compiled lists. However, names that appear on mail-order lists represent people who have purchased, or inquired about, a specific product or service. This action identifies them as mail-order buyers, regardless of the media type that served as the stimulus.

Mail-order lists can also be divided into broad classifications, such as gift buyers, opportunity seekers, self-improvement enthusiasts, book buyers, magazine subscribers, buyers of office supplies, and financial service buyers. Descriptions of every list available on the market appear on data cards published by list brokers (companies that arrange for rental of all types of lists) and *Direct Mail Lists Rates & Data,* published semi-annually by Standard Rates & Data Service (SRDS). A typical data card is reproduced on the facing page.

Difference Between Mail-Order and Compiled Lists

The major difference between mail-order and compiled lists is that the former group usually outperforms the latter in terms of response. The difference stems primarily from the following three characteristics:

- People whose names appear on mail-order lists have demonstrated a propensity to buy by mail. Those on compiled lists have not.
- Mail-order lists can be selected on the basis of psychographics as reflected by the products or services purchased. Compiled lists cannot.
- Mail-order lists have a significantly greater incidence of "readers," since most direct marketing offers are made in print.

Compiled lists are usually the vehicles of choice in situations in which a high level of penetration within restricted geographic areas is desired, for example, retailers who need to reach an audience in a limited trading area to build store traffic, and companies seeking leads for salesmen in concentrated sales areas.

XYZ LEATHER GOODS

	MEN	WOMEN	TOTAL	
BUYERS:	73,046	366,862	439,908 Hotline	$ 5.00 M Ex.
	167,149	905,160	1,072,309 1976	30.00 M
	229,466	931,312	1,159,778 1975	30.00 M

*CANADIAN:

248,600		1976	35.00 M
69,200		Late 1975	35.00 M

CATALOG BUYERS:	PLEASE INQUIRE	5.00 M Ex.
CREDIT CARD NAMES:	PLEASE INQUIRE	10.00 M Ex.

DIRECT MAIL SOURCE NAMES:

51,511	258,454	309,965 Hotline	5.00 M Ex.
125,313	644,930	770,243 1976	35.00 M
164,197	600,032	764,229 1975	35.00

OTHER SOURCE NAMES (NOT DIRECT MAIL OR T.V.):

21,535	108,408	139,943 Hotline	5.00 M Ex.
41,836	260,230	302,066 1976	25.00 M
64,269	331,280	395,549 1975	25.00 M

#1981 April 1977

SEX: See Counts: *Mostly Women; (80% Women); Sex Selec. Avail. @ N/C

ARRANGEMENT:
Zip Code Sequence; State Selec. Avail. @ $2.00 M Ex.; SCF Selec. Avail. @ $3.50 M Ex.; Zip Selec. Avail. @ $5.00 M Extra

ADDRESSING:
5-Across Cheshire; Magnetic Tape; Press. Sens. Avail. @ $1.50 M Ex.; Key Coding Avail. @ 50¢ M Ex.

LIST SELECTION

List selection is a science combined with art and the instincts of a Mississippi riverboat gambler. Hundreds of lists are available from compilers and list brokers. Obviously, it is impractical and uneconomical to test every one of them, or even every name appearing on one list, to find those that will produce sufficient income to meet the cost/value criteria. The marketer, therefore, is faced with two problems: (1) to select only those *lists* that have a good chance of success, and (2) to select only those *segments of lists* that have a good chance of success. Here we will deal with the first problem. Segmentation techniques are discussed later.

There are two ways of selecting lists: by classification and by individual characteristics, both of which are applicable both to mail-order and compiled lists.

Mail-Order Lists

Selection by Classification

Mail-order lists are classified by the product or service purchased and, in some cases, by business, profession, and so on, examples of which might be buyers of business supplies, cheese, factory janitorial supplies, and self-improvement services. Their *selection by the classification method* is based on the principle that if a list of a certain classification proves successful, others of the same classification are also likely to do so. For example, the successful use of a list of buyers of a course in interior decorating for the sale of life insurance serves as the trigger to test other lists of buyers of self-improvement products or services for the sale of life insurance. List brokers typically operate on this premise. They recommend those list classifications that have worked for marketers of similar or competitive offers to companies entering the direct mail field for the first time, as well as to their regular customers.

Not all lists of the same classification will perform equally well, however. The weakness of the method of selection by classification lies in the fact that not all lists of the same classification have the same characteristics. For example, one list of gift buyers may have been developed through space advertising in *The New Yorker* and the other through *The Rotarian*.

Selection by Individual Characteristics

This weakness can be overcome through selection by characteristics, which takes into account demographic and psychographic characteristics of the buyers as well as features of the list itself, such as recency, monetary values, and media source.

Lists have many characteristics. Some have no effect on response, and others have negative or positive effects. Here are the characteristics that usually have an impact on response:

Demographic Characteristics	List Characteristics
Age	Recency
Sex	Monetary Value
Income	Media source
Social status	Inquirers/Buyers
Occupational class	
Product class	

Application of statistical techniques, such as multiple regression analysis, to response data of lists already used, measures the impact of each characteristic on response. It can be used to predict the response on lists being considered for inclusion in a test mailing. Only those lists whose predicted response is in line with the cost/value criteria are selected.

Besides its value as a predictive tool, the individual-characteristic method allows the marketer to test lists he or she would not consider under the classification method. When introduced by the authors about 20 years ago, the success-to-failure ratio of lists rose from what was then considered a respectable 4 : 10 to 8 : 10. The number of lists tested was, of course, reduced, but so were the test budget and losses.

Unfortunately, the method requires about one year of company experience with mail-order lists before it can be used. In the meantime, lists can be selected by using good judgment buttressed with the following generalizations about characteristics:

Recency, More recently acquired names perform better.

Monetary value, Other things remaining constant, performance improves as the unit of sale rises.

Media source, Performance improves as the incidence of customers acquired through direct mail solicitations increases. Performance worsens as the incidence of customers acquired through other media increases. The declining rank order of other media is as follows: magazines, newspapers, TV, radio, all others.

Product class, Response increases in direct proportion to the closeness of relationship between products or service formerly purchased and currently offered.

Inquirers/Buyers, Buyers perform better than inquirers.

The effect of the other characteristics on response depends on the demographic makeup of your market. For example, a list of upper-middle-class people is likely to perform well if your product appeals to that social class.

Compiled Lists

The consumer household compilation involves selecting groups of names on the basis of individual characteristics and employing list segmentation techniques, which will be discussed subsequently. Other compilations lend themselves more easily to the classification selection method because compilers, anticipating user needs, have segmented broad classes of compilations into smaller, more homogeneous units. One marketer, for example, whose product or service has wide appeal among doctors may select a list of all doctors. A second marketer, whose product or service can be used only by those in private practice, will select that group alone, or any other group by specialty. Each segment is available as a list entity. Similarly, business and industry lists are available by Standard Industrial Classification (SIC) code, teachers by subject and grade level, and so forth.

Use of the individual-characteristic method in the selection of compiled lists involves the selection of subclassifications. Here again compilers have anticipated user needs and compiled names from major classifications on the basis of one or two characteristics to create lists, such as corporations employing 50 to 100 persons, sixth-grade teachers and so forth.

LIST SEGMENTATION

List segmentation techniques are used to select prospects whose demographic/psychographic profile identifies them as prime prospects for the product or service offered. As in list selection, different methods are used to select segments of mail-order and compiled lists.

Mail-Order Lists

As pointed out earlier, people whose names appear on mail-order lists share certain socioeconomic/psychographic characteristics. Each mail-order list represents a segment of the total universe to which it belongs. For example, buyers of office supplies constitute a segment of the business universe, and buyers of kitchen gadgets are a segment of the consumer household universe.

Other factors are at work within each list as well. Some tend to improve performance, others to worsen it. A prime consideration is that while everyone on the list shares certain characteristics, they do not have all in common. Hence, response performance is adversely affected by those who do not have the chief characteristics associated with the purchase of your product or service. Performance of mail-order lists can be improved significantly by identifying those names from the entire list that are most likely to have the required characteristics. This can be achieved by employing list segmentation techniques, such as segmentation by *duplication* and by *geography* (regional, state, metro area, county, ZIP Code, census tract, or block group).

Segmentation by duplication operates on the principle that names appearing on more than one mail-order list have certain things in common and that, when combined, they create one list that has many things in common. Here is a simplified example of how to use segmentation by duplication when the goal is to come up with a list of people who have three characteristics in common.

Assume that a marketer has found that the most responsive lists consist of people who have bought a kitchen appliance or home decorating item in the $20 to $50 price range in response to direct-mail solicitations and who have a median income of $17,500. Assume further that three lists are available, none of which meets all the criteria, but each of which meets one of them. Table 2A illustrates the information contained in List X, which consists of buyers of a cutlery set at $24.95 offered in magazine space ads; List Y, people who have asked for and received a free catalog on indoor

Table 2. Segmented markets.

A. Characteristics of Three Lists

	List X		List Y		List Z	
List type	=	Customers	=	Inquirers	=	Compiled
Medium	=	Magazine space ad	=	Co-op direct mail	=	Directories
Item	=	Cutlery set	=	Plant accessories	=	None
Unit of sale	=	$24.95	=	$0	=	$0
Median income	=	Mixed	=	Mixed	=	$17,500

B. Computer-Run Comparisons

Duplicates Between X and Y

List types	=	Buyers and inquirers
Media	=	Magazine space ad and direct mail
Item	=	Home related
Unit of sale	=	$24.95
Median income	=	Mixed

Duplicates Between X and Z

List types	=	Customers
Media	=	Magazine space ad and directories
Item	=	Home related
Unit of sale	=	$24.95
Median income	=	$17,500

Duplicates Among X, Y, and Z

List types	=	Customers and inquirers
Media	=	Magazine space ad, direct mail, and directories
Item	=	Home related
Unit of sale	=	$24.95
Median income	=	$17,500

plant accessories costing from $18 to $40 in response to a co-op direct mail solicitation within the past year, but who have made no purchase; and List Z, a compilation of households with a median income of $17,500.

None of the three contains a group of people with a history of buying in response to direct mail solicitations. However, names that are duplicated on all three lists meet all the criteria specified: List X, buyers of home-related items by mail; List Y, a history of responding to direct mail offers; and List Z, a median income of $17,500. Duplicates are identified by running the three lists against each other in a compare routine on computer. Table 2B shows the results of the run: duplication between X and Y; between Y and Z; and among X, Y, and Z. The last-mentioned combination is composed of those names that meet the three criteria for selection.

Multibuyers (customers of more than one company, who therefore appear on more than one mail-order list) are segmented by means of the same compare routine. Multibuyers are more likely to buy by mail. Selection by duplication can also be used to select inactive names on a house list whose reactivation is most likely to be profitable. Typically, direct marketers conduct mailings to inactive customers until the response rate becomes unprofitable. People discontinue buying for a number of reasons: They've moved and third-class bulk mail no longer reaches them; family maturation eliminates need or desire for products offered; they've had poor experience with mail-order buying.

Not all inactive customers are alike. Some are more inactive than others. One way to identify those who are less inactive is to compare the house list inactives with mail-order prospect lists. Assuming that the prospect names have been acquired recently, duplicates between the customer prospect lists and the house list inactives are most likely to buy again and be more profitable over time, since duplicated names are buying from another company. Efforts directed toward this group are usually more profitable than are those aimed at the total inactive universe of the house list.

Geographic selection is based on the fact that certain areas of the country have proved more responsive than others. The level of responsiveness is a product of the geographic proximity to the company, the product, or the service offered and the demographic/psychographic characteristics of a geographic area. The purpose of geographic segmentation is to identify which geographic units are most responsive to your company and to your product or service. The responsive units can be identified in one of three ways: (1) analyzing previously used prospect lists, (2) analyzing the house list, (3) testing.

The previously used prospect lists can be analyzed if the list owners have furnished counts by geographic units. Such counts are furnished when requested. The first step is to compare the number of pieces mailed from all prospect lists into each geographic unit with the number of responses from each unit, then to convert the response into a percentage of the pieces mailed. The percentage figures can be used to construct an index so that those units with the higher index numbers constitute the prime market areas. Besides identifying the specific geographic units with high-performance levels from among those used, the data can also be employed to select other geographic units that are likely to perform well. This is accomplished by developing a demographic profile of the high-performance units and selecting other units with matching profiles.

The house-list analysis method consists of obtaining a count of names from each geographic unit on the house list and converting it into a percentage of the total households in the unit. All other procedures are the same as those used in analyzing prospect lists, as discussed earlier. This method is less reliable than analyzing prospect lists, however, because the number of names on the house list from any one geographic unit is a function of the number of pieces mailed. Nevertheless, it will serve the purpose for the time being, until it is possible to use the prospect-list analysis method or the testing procedure outline.

Testing to identify high-performance units involves first selecting geographic units by the best-judgment method, making sure that each region of the country is included, and then selecting segments of mail-order lists representing the selected units and mailing an offer to the names selected. Response to the mailing is converted to a percentage of the number of pieces mailed to each unit, and an index is constructed as outlined earlier.

Compiled Lists

It has been pointed out that the consumer household universe encompasses virtually every household in the country and that no marketer needs or wants to reach so diverse a universe. It was also pointed out that compilations of other universes (business, industry, professional) are available as list entities on the basis of one or two characteristics, and can therefore be selected by employing the classification method. Each of these factors influences the methods used in selecting segments of the various universes. The discussion of segmenting compiled lists can be divided into two categories: segmentation of the consumer household compilation, and segmentation of all other compilations.

Consumer household compilations can be segmented into various demographic units by applying U.S. Census Bureau socioeconomic data of each ZIP Code, census tract, or block group (audience cell) to each address falling within one of those geographic units. In addition, compilers can identify specific households on the basis of the number of years occupied by the same family, number of cars owned by make and model year, and other characteristics not available from census data.

The highest level of demographic homogeneity among residents is found in block groups, since these units contain about 250 households. Census tracts, with about 1,000 households, offer the second highest degree of homogeneity. ZIP Codes, which sometimes encompass an entire county and as many as 10,000 households, offer the least.

A marketer may order a list of any number of households by specifying the geographic areas or by outlining the socioeconomic profile desired. In the former case, all names in those areas selected will be supplied. In the latter, all names (or a sample) in those units meeting the profile will be selected. It is important to understand that each name does not meet the profile, since socioeconomic parameters for each Census Bureau unit are reported as averages and medians, not as absolutes for each household.

Segmentation of the consumer household universe is based on the selection of Census Bureau geographic units whose residents meet predetermined demographic criteria. The first step is to establish the demographic criteria. A profile of the house list will serve as a guide for selecting them or, in its absence, best judgment. A house-list profile can be developed in either of two ways:

- Mailing questionnaires or conducting field interviews, using a random sample of the house list.
- Assigning to all households on the house list the demographic characteristics of the Census Bureau geographic unit

in which they are located (ZIP Code, census tract, block group).

Of the two methods, the first is more reliable because it will reveal whether the customers are typical or atypical members of the areas in which they live. The profile is used as a basis for the selection of geographic units with matching characteristics that have a significant impact on response. However, the weakness inherent in this procedure is the fact that the house-list profile is a function of the media vehicles used in building the list. Hence, the profile is skewed with regard to a number of characteristics, the most important of which is the high incidence of people with a propensity to buy by mail. Other characteristics affected in this way include income, occupational class, number of children, discretionary spending power, and a number of psychographic characteristics. Selection of compiled list segments can be made only on the basis of demographic criteria. Psychographics can only be assumed by relating them to certain demographics.

The weakness inherent in the procedure can be overcome by adjusting the profile to compensate for the differences in, or absence of, characteristics. For example: The house-list profile shows an average of 1.9 children under 18 in customer households, and you know that this characteristic has a significant impact on response. The question raised by this is, whether response can be improved by selecting units in which the average number of children under 18 is fewer than 1.9 or more than that. There is no way to answer the question judgmentally. It can be answered by testing geographic units with fewer than 1.9, with more than 1.9, and with 1.9. The result, as measured by response as a percentage of total households in the unit, may show that the lower number is better than the higher number. This incidence of children demonstrates that the absence of other characteristics in the compilation can be compensated for by a downward adjustment in the average number of children. Hence, units with fewer than 1.9 children per household should be selected for the rollout.

The consumer household compilation should be used only after the supply of suitable mail-order lists has been exhausted, or the number of names available from them is too low to achieve growth objectives. In most cases, it is more profitable to use selected segments of marginally productive mail-order lists than to use segments of the consumer household compilation.

Other compilations of industrial, professional, educational, and similar groups are available by classification or on the basis of one or two characteristics. In many cases, compilers, for a price, will provide smaller segments of the compilations by tailoring selection to a user's requirements. The segments can be selected geographically or by individual characteristics.

Typically, segments selected are related to the product or service offered. For example, a manufacturer of sausage casings wishes to reach sausage makers in eight midwest states each of whose total annual production is 5 tons or more. The compilation of the meat-packing universe consists of 8,500 plants, 3,500 of which are sausage manufacturers. Of those 3,500, 1,800 are in the eight midwest states, and of those only 700 produce 5 tons or more of sausage. A compiler can provide the names of the 700 manufacturers needed.

USES OF LISTS

The most common use of lists involves solo mailings, in which one seller offers one product or service. The mailing package usually consists of four elements: letter, flyer (brochure), reply (order) form, and business reply envelope, all of which are inserted in a carrier (outside) envelope. Other uses of prospect lists and of a house list are co-op mailings, package inserts, syndication, and house-list rental.

Co-op Mailings

Opportunities to participate in co-op mailings typically are offered by owners of compiled lists. Offers from a number of companies are inserted in one mailing package. This has become one of the more popular media vehicles for distributing cents-off coupons.

Co-ops are more effective in offering products or services that lend themselves to simple description, since the space available is limited by the size and weight of the paper stock permitted. The cost per thousand is relatively low because all participants share in the cost of the list, insertion, carrier envelope, mailing services, and postage. This lower cost is reflected, however, in lower response levels. Participation should be based on the cost per order criterion. Co-op mailings are available on a national and local level.

Special-interest co-ops aimed at target markets are also available. Examples are newlyweds, new parents, new occupants, armed forces, industries, and businesses by type, professional disciplines, and so on. Co-ops are usually addressed to "occupant" or "resident."

Package Inserts

Package inserts are offers by one seller inserted in the fulfillment package of another. Typically, the offer is made using a solo direct mail package or a catalog. The major advantages of package inserts are that (1) the mailer saves the cost of postage, (2) the people reached are the most recent buyers. The major disadvantages are (1) that the number of prospects reached is limited to the number of orders fulfilled over any given time span and (2) seasonal variations.

Most orders are shipped just before Christmas in many product categories. Hence, an offer will usually reach many prospects when it is too late to place an order for Christmas goods. One can adjust for this factor by using package inserts in those packages of sellers whose products are shipped during an earlier season. Package inserts are an added source of profit for a company with a direct marketing operation since it can offer sellers of noncompeting products space in its fulfillment packages.

Syndication

Syndication describes a situation in which a list owner makes a mailing to his or her customers under his company name offering the product or service of another. The implied endorsement by the mailer is the rationale behind syndication. It is a valid rationale, for it does increase response. The product offered is unrelated to the company's main business. Examples are product offerings by oil companies and credit card issuers, such as American Express. Some chain retailers have found this to be a source of extra profits by using their lists of credit customers.

The syndicator (i.e., the person who owns the product) usually assumes all the financial risks involved and compensates the list owner for the use of the list and company endorsement. Compensation can take the form of a flat fee or a percentage of gross sales. The list owning company can increase its compensation by assuming more of the risk.

House-List Rental

Once a company owns a mail-order list, it can derive a significant profit from renting that list to other direct marketing companies. The rental fee covers the use of the list for one time only. Rentals are arranged through list brokers. The use of your list by another, noncompetitive direct marketer does not adversely affect response to your offer.

CATALOGS

Catalogs are the most widely used medium for soliciting repeat sales from customers. However, they are fraught with danger to the financial health of an enterprise. Production of a catalog is frequently considered an essential first step in setting up a direct marketing operation. This is where the danger lies. It is wiser to hold off publication of a catalog until the number of names available on the house list is large enough to effect economies of scale needed for economical production and distribution. There are exceptions to this rule, but not many.

Preparation of Catalogs

Preparation of catalogs involves the diverse talents of a photographer, a layout artist, a merchandiser, a copywriter, etc. Each contributes his or her special talent and technical knowledge to the job. The end product should be a catalog that will create a buying atmosphere for the prospect. The more important factors that go into the preparation of a catalog are described below.

A *theme* should be established for the catalog. One way to do this is to give it a name, such as "Christmas Gifts for the Home," "Wholesale Auto Parts," or "Spring Fashion Values."

Allocation of space is determined by the cost per page. Hence, one must determine the space cost and ask how much would be spent in other types of print media to promote the product. No more should be "spent" in the catalog. The catalog space cost is charged to each product. A sales analysis shows the profitability of each item. This may lead to an increase or decrease of the space allotted to each product or its elimination from the catalog. In all cases, sufficient space must be reserved to fully describe the product and, if necessary, show it in use. Illustrations of people quickly convey the dimensions of products and add interest.

Product position is related to expected sales. The most popular and profitable products are featured on the front and back covers, on the two inside covers, and before and after order forms. The front of the book is reserved for the next most popular group of items, and so forth.

Adding new products ranks among the merchandiser's bigger problems. No matter how enthusiastic you are about a new product, it should not be added to the line until it has been tested. There are a number of methods that can be used for testing. One is to run a series of small space ads in high-performance media vehicles featuring one or two items in each. This method could reduce financial risk and provide sales data that may determine the use of the items in the catalog. Solo direct mail packages, each featuring one or two items, and a mini catalog consisting of all promising items are two other testing devices. In each case, the piece is mailed to a small sample of the house list.

Color will enhance the overall appearance of the catalog and increase sales, especially when color is an essential ingredient in making product selection. Cost should be related to the increase in sales resulting from the use of color. If sales rise 75 percent with process color, but the cost eats up all the additional profit, color becomes prohibitive. The opposite, of course, is also true. If the cost of process color is prohibitive, consider using it only in one or two signatures and/or covers. There one may display products whose sales volume is affected by color. The other signatures can be printed in one or two flat colors, using tints, duotones, flat-tint halftones, and other tricks in the graphic designer's bag.

Distribution Criteria and Methods

Assuming that the house list is large enough to take advantage of the economies of scale, two methods are used to broaden distribution beyond the house list: Offer a catalog free or for a minimal sum (try to cover postage and production costs) in small-space advertising in selected magazines (classified ads are frequently effective), and offer a specific product in space ads and insert the catalog in the fulfillment package to buyers. Both methods can easily be combined in one ad.

It is important to maintain accurate records of the buying activity of each catalog recipient. Unless yours is a very unusual case, it will be found that those who receive a catalog after making a purchase will be the most productive, those who pay for it will be the second most productive, and those who receive it free will be the least productive. The purpose of maintaining records is not to discover which of the three groups is most productive, but to determine which of the methods of catalog distribution meet the customer cost/value criteria. It is possible that even the least productive group will meet these criteria.

3

The Future
of Direct Marketing

DOES the future of direct marketing lie in electronic shopping, in which the telephone, the computer, and television play leading roles? Will retail stores be replaced by distribution centers from which goods will be shipped directly to homes and offices? Will print media give way to cable television piped into homes equipped with communication/entertainment centers? Will workers, occupied at their jobs during the day and too tired to endure traffic and crowds in the evening, shop from their homes by pressing buttons? Although the required technology to bring about such a future is now in place in test markets in various parts of the country, the answers to those questions are still under debate between technocrats and behaviorists.

In this section, we introduce the reader to electronic shopping by outlining some of its principal features and by presenting some of the arguments on both sides of the debate that is raging between the technocrats, who believe the future will be here soon, and the behaviorists, who remain skeptical. Those who plan to adopt direct marketing methods should be aware of what the future may look like since the outcome of the debate and the tests is likely to have an impact on their plans.

BEHAVIORISTS vs. TECHNOCRATS

At the core of the debate is the age-old question of public acceptance. Technocrats point to historical precedents to support their view that technology will be used for the same reason that men climb mountains — it's there. And it's there now. In contrast, the major point of the behaviorists is that it takes more than available technology to usher in the future. However, direct marketers, who are behaviorists in their own right, see the seeds of electronic shopping in the recent growth of their businesses. They maintain that the sharp increase in the number of working women and older people is responsible for a significant part of that growth. The method is already accepted, only the media will change.

Behaviorists are convinced that if the kind of change envisioned by electronic shopping eventually is to be accepted, it will first to be adopted by a well-educated and adventurous young population. They point out that by the 1980s or the 1990s America will be dominated by the 41 million persons born in the post-World War II baby boom. By that date, this segment of the population will have reached their middle years, and their behavior patterns will be solidly entrenched. It is possible that the values of the middle-aged baby boom cohort, including their willing acceptance of change, may usher in widespread use of direct marketing through electronic media. Moreover, many contend that because of their demographic characteristics the values of this cohort will continue to influence the mores of the nation into the next century. The baby boomers' view of parenthood, for instance, will produce a population dominated by older people during the balance of this century. And in the absence of another baby boom before 1982 (the date at which the eldest women of the baby boom will be well into their fertile years), the projected population of 2040 will reach what demographers call a stabilized age structure, the point at which all generation and age groups are about the same size. The median age will continue to rise from its present 27 to 35 by the year 2000, and to 37 by 2030. Although the youth population of the future — the children of the baby boomers — is expected to decline as a percentage of the total population, because the fertility rate is now less than half what it was at the peak of the baby boom, they nevertheless will constitute a significant force in absolute number —

some 25 million over the next 10 to 15 years, according to current estimates. When they reach shopping age, electronic shopping may be just as routine to them as the supermarkets and discount stores are to their parents today.

How valid is the behaviorists' contention that change is accepted by the young and well educated? As evidence marketers trace the development of supermarkets and discount stores. The parents of the baby boomers accepted these outlets first in postwar California, where the population was younger and better educated. The trend jumped across the country to the East Coast, and then made its way inland from both coasts. Acceptance came with some reluctance as the postwar population shifted to the suburbs where shopping centers replaced neighborhood stores. Today, while the baby boomers shop supermarkets and other self-service stores as a matter of routine, their parents still fondly recall the corner grocery and meat market of their childhood.

In contrast, the skeptics say that as the baby boomers age, they too are likely to resist change. As evidence, they cite the baby boomers' reluctance to accept both electronic funds transfer in place of the plastic credit card, which was more than a generation in gaining acceptance, and electronic check-out readers, which are being introduced in supermarkets. Will the baby boomers accept electronic shopping only reluctantly as their mothers accepted the supermarket?

In addition to the divided views of behaviorists, there are cost considerations which some say will be the determining factor. Advocates of advanced electronic marketing techniques contend that available technology will be put to use, not so much because it is there (like the mountain peak beckoning to the climber), but because the escalating costs of traditional advertising and distribution will favor more advanced and less costly methods. Supporting this argument, the technocrats maintain that when the cost/benefit ratio becomes favorable, marketers will be encouraged to adopt the new technology. And, they add, if there is any validity to the behaviorists' assertion that acceptance of change is related to education, the highly educated baby-boom population is most likely to accept the change. To clinch the argument, technologists add that for a generation born with a telephone attached to its ears, a television screen glued to its eyes, and computers recording its lives, acceptance of electronic shopping should be easy.

HOW IT WORKS

What is electronic shopping like? Cable TV is at its core. The multiplicity of 30 or more available channels and the two-way communication capability of the touch-tone telephone together with voice-activated computers make it possible for marketers to beam their offers at sharply defined market segments. Unlike commercial TV, cable TV has a list of subscribers whose demographic profile is readily available.

People can tune to specific stations at certain times to shop for certain items. People who want to buy clothing can tune to the station showing items at their favorite store. If nothing catches their eye, they can tune to another station transmitting fashion items from another store. If the stores aren't showing what they want, perhaps they can find something in a "catalog," a tape played through the TV screen. And if that doesn't work, the customer may call a computer at the store across town or across the country and ask to see what it has to offer. The computer answers by playing an appropriate voice drum and then showing what's in stock. The customer doesn't have to wait in line because the computer can handle hundreds of requests simultaneously. A person shops when it's convenient — 24 hours a day, seven days a week, holidays included, even in areas where blue laws still exist.

Test marketing of new products takes a few hours instead of a few weeks or months. Marketers need only show a product on the screen and ask for orders. They can program statistical techniques into the computer to learn whether the product will sell in sufficient quantity to allow them to include it in their line — all from one exposure. The ebb and flow of audience interest is measured by meters attached to individual sets. When the audience size begins to fall, the marketer can show something else or ask the audience what it would like to see.

A running account of what's selling and what's not is maintained on a minute-by-minute basis by the computer, which digests sales data and communicates re-orders directly to suppliers' computers without interrupting communication with its own customers. Merchandise is moved in and out of inventory by computer-command automated equipment, which picks orders, packs them, and sends them on their way to customers, computing the shipping and packing costs as it does so.

This is not a description of the future as viewed by a looney inventor sitting in a patent attorney's reception room with blueprints under arm. It is the view of those who have developed the hardware and software and who are investing money and talent in tests. In this respect, the future is here. It awaits public acceptance.

REFERENCES

FOOTNOTES

1. Stone, Bob, "When and Where to Mail," *Advertising Age,* Jan. 5, 1970, p. 37.
2. Kobs, Jim, "99 Direct Response Offers That Can Improve Results," *Direct Marketing,* Oct. 1975, pp. 24-42.
3. Fenvessy, Stanley J., *Importance of Fulfillment in Keeping Customers Happy,* Manual Release No. 1401. (New York: Direct Mail/Marketing Association, Jan. 1976.)

SELECTED READINGS

Bair, Martin, "Complex Marketing Activities Bring. Need for Segmentation," *Direct Marketing,* Jan. 1976, pp. 36-43.

Barn, Christian, *Direct Mail and Direct Response Promotion.* (London: Kogan Page, 1971.)

Fernandes, Richard L., *Financial Direct Response Advertising.* (Staten Island, N.Y., Feddes Enterprises, 1975.)

Hodgson, Richard S., *Direct Mail & Mail Order Handbook.* (Chicago: The Dartnell Corporation, 1964.)

Jain, Chaman L., "Newspaper Advertising Response: Preprint Vs. R.O.P.," *Journal of Advertising Research,* Aug. 1973, pp. 30-32.

_____, "Effectiveness of Broadcast Support to Newspaper Ads," *Journal of Advertising Research,* Oct. 1975, pp. 69-72.

_____, and Migliaro, A., "Optimum Customer Investment in Mail Order

Operation," *Atlanta Economic Review,* July/Aug. 1973, pp. 45-47.

Mayer, Edward N., Jr., and Ljungren, Roy G. (Ed.), *The Handbook Of Industrial Direct Mail Advertising.* (New York: Business/Professional Advertising Association, 1972.)

Migliaro, A., and Jain, Chaman L., *Direct Mail Econometrics: The Scientific Approach to Successful Marketing by Mail,* Parts I–III. (Washington, D.C.: Mail Marketing Associates, 1964, 1965.)

Stone, Bob, *Successful Direct Marketing Methods.* (Chicago: Crain Books, 1975.)

FUTURISTIC READINGS

Here is a list of articles on the future of direct marketing that have appeared, in just one magazine, since 1970.

Adler, John, "CATV Joins Communication Revolution to Aid Marketers," *Direct Marketers,* Apr. 1971, pp. 28-32.

Bride, Edward J., "Marketers Will Have to Face Brave New Marketing World," *Direct Marketing,* May 1975, pp. 26-35.

Campbell, Alastair M., "Coming Alliance: Direct Marketing: CATV Cassettes," *Direct Marketing,* Jan. 1972, pp. 36-46.

Carpenter, Marshall, Jr., "Buck Rogers Is Here: Push Button Ordering Techniques," *Direct Marketing,* Oct. 1973, pp. 122-165.

Guzfosky, Elliot, "Direct Marketing Moves into New Channels with CATV Boom," Interview, *Direct Marketing,* Mar. 1973, pp. 25-37.

Kamen, Ira, "Link to the Future: Cable TV Provides New Marketing Tool," *Direct Marketing,* July 1972, pp. 41-48.

Lane, Ken, "Automated Telephone Service Brings Store to Customers," *Direct Marketing,* Apr. 1974, pp. 68-87.

Nathanson, Marc, "Cable Television Future Coupled with Direct Mail," *Direct Marketing,* July 1975, pp. 40-43.

Nebenzahl, Paul, "Computer Picture for Retail Marketing Plans," *Direct Marketing,* Dec. 1970, pp. 26-32.

Schlafly, H. J., "Teleprompter in Vanguard of CATV Engineering Development," *Direct Marketing,* Apr. 1971, pp. 43-50.